OVERCOMING ADVERSITY:
SHARING THE AMERICAN DREAM

JOHNNY DEPP

MASON CREST PUBLISHERS
PHILADELPHIA

OVERCOMING ADVERSITY:
SHARING THE AMERICAN DREAM

Charles Barkley
Halle Berry
Cesar Chavez
Kenny Chesney
George Clooney
Johnny Depp
Tony Dungy
Jermaine Dupri
Jennifer Garner
Kevin Garnett
John B. Herrington
Salma Hayek
Vanessa Hudgens
Samuel L. Jackson

Norah Jones
Martin Lawrence
Bruce Lee
Eva Longoria
Malcolm X
Carlos Mencia
Chuck Norris
Barack Obama
Rosa Parks
Bill Richardson
Russell Simmons
Carrie Underwood
Modern American
  Indian Leaders

OVERCOMING ADVERSITY:
SHARING THE AMERICAN DREAM

JOHNNY DEPP

BILL WINE

MASON CREST PUBLISHERS
PHILADELPHIA

ABOUT CROSS-CURRENTS

When you see this logo, turn to the Cross-Currents section at the back of the book. The Cross-Currents features explore connections between people, places, events, and ideas.

Produced by OTTN Publishing, Stockton, New Jersey

Mason Crest Publishers
370 Reed Road
Broomall, PA 19008
www.masoncrest.com

First printing

1 3 5 7 9 8 6 4 2

Library of Congress Cataloging-in-Publication Data

Wine, Bill.
   Johnny Depp / Bill Wine.
      p. cm. — (Sharing the American dream : overcoming adversity)
   Includes bibliographical references.
   ISBN 978-1-4222-0593-8 (hardcover) — ISBN 978-1-4222-0742-0 (pbk.)
  1. Depp, Johnny—Juvenile literature. 2. Motion picture actors and actresses—United States—Biography—Juvenile literature. I. Title.
   PN2287.D39W56 2008
   791.4302'8092273—dc22
                                        2008024540

OVERCOMING ADVERSITY:
SHARING THE AMERICAN DREAM

TABLE OF CONTENTS

CHAPTER ONE

OSCAR-WORTHY

On January 27, 2004, actor Johnny Depp was surprised to hear his name among the nominations for one of the film industry's most coveted awards—the Oscar. The Academy of Motion Picture Arts and Sciences gives the honor annually in recognition of the best movies, performances, and related work from the past year. At the January 27, 2004, press conference announcing the nominees for the 2003 Academy Awards, Johnny's name was the first mentioned in the Best Actor category. He had been nominated for his performance in the 2003 film *Pirates of the Caribbean: The Curse of the Black Pearl*.

Why?

The news of his first Oscar nomination shocked the popular actor. Johnny was so surprised, in fact, that his first response was "Why?" *Pirates of the Caribbean* was a lighthearted, humorous take on the pirate adventures of cinema's past—not the usual fare to earn big awards. In the film, Depp had played Captain Jack Sparrow, the smirking rogue buccaneer who drives the plot and pleases the audience. Depp questioned whether his role of the offbeat pirate, while clever and entertaining, was indeed worthy of an Oscar. "On one level I was flattered," Depp

Johnny Depp and longtime girlfriend Vanessa Paradis attend the Academy Awards held in Hollywood, California, on February 29, 2004.

told Erik Hedegaard of *Rolling Stone.* "But it's not what I'm working for."

The other award nominees had turned in much more serious performances. Ben Kingsley was nominated for the drama *House of Sand and Fog,* in which he starred as a man who fights to save his family's home. In *Cold Mountain* Jude Law had played a Confederate soldier who leaves the battlefield to return to his love. Usually known for his comic roles, Bill Murray played an actor filming a commercial in Japan who develops an unlikely relationship with a younger woman in *Lost in Translation.* Nominated three times previously for an Academy Award, Sean Penn was up for his role as the father of a murdered girl in the drama *Mystic River.*

READ MORE

The golden statuette known as the Oscar is an award coveted by actors, producers, directors, and many others in the film industry. For some background information on the history of American film's biggest award, turn to page 46.

Crazy About Captain Jack

The Pirates of the Caribbean was a comedic fantasy thriller loosely based on a Disney theme park ride of the same name. During shooting, Johnny had played main character Captain Jack Sparrow in a way that had worried some of the studio executives at Walt Disney Pictures. Depp reportedly based Captain Jack on guitarist Keith Richards of the Rolling Stones. Johnny also borrowed from the Warner Bros. Studio's Looney Tunes cartoon skunk, Pepé Le Pew. The film's director, Gore Verbinski, has said that he believes the

READ MORE

To learn more about Pepé Le Pew, the cartoon character who helped inspire Johnny's characterization of Captain Jack Sparrow, turn to page 47.

Johnny poses with Rolling Stones guitarist Keith Richards, who served as inspiration for the character of Jack Sparrow in *The Pirates of the Caribbean*. Richards later appeared with Johnny in one of the film's sequels.

"reel-life" character of Sparrow closely resembles Depp's real-life personality.

Johnny was aware of the studio executives' misgivings about how he was playing Jack Sparrow. But he refused to change anything. It turned out that there was no need for the studio execs to worry. The audiences loved the film, and often cited Depp's character as the reason why.

Released on July 9, 2003, *Pirates of Caribbean: The Curse of the Black Pearl* raked in more than $70 million at the box office in just five days. Hollywood insiders had long thought that pirate movies were a thing of the past, but Depp and the rest of the cast proved them wrong.

An Unusual Actor

Long before *Pirates of the Caribbean*, Depp had already established a reputation as an actor who was quirky and unpredictable, but unfailingly interesting. Critics had praised his acting abilities. And he had shown that he could handle all genres—or types—of films. His movies had included horror thrillers, historical dramas, romantic fantasies, science fiction dramas, and slapstick comedies.

However, despite being admired by both movie reviewers and fans, Johnny did not appear in many films that produced big-ticket sales. Although he had starred in about two-dozen movies, Johnny hadn't reached Hollywood's A-list. (The A-list refers to the actors whose presence in a movie almost guarantees the film's success at the box office.)

Although Johnny was not yet considered the kind of star who was a proven hit maker, directors sought to work with him because of his ability. Entertainment journalists often referred to him as a "best actor of his generation" candidate. And he had actually turned down a number of lead roles in big-budget mass-appeal movies that had gone on to become blockbusters.

Johnny was careful about the roles he would take because he wanted to maintain control over his image. Earlier in his career, from 1987 to 1990, he had been a teen heartthrob on the television show *21 Jump Street*. And he had been extremely uncomfortable in that role of teenage idol. In fact, Depp often told reporters that he felt he had been "forced into the role of 'product.'"

One of Johnny's *21 Jump Street* promotional photos. He disliked his "teen idol" status and was determined to play more serious roles.

To counter that image, Johnny had developed a reputation as a bad boy. He engaged in some outrageous exploits off-screen that landed him regularly in celebrity magazines. That reputation did nothing to advance his career. It had taken him years to become viewed as a serious actor, and not just another handsome face.

And the Winner Is . . .

On February 22, a week before the 2004 Academy Awards ceremony, Depp won the Screen Actors Guild Award for Best Actor. His victory was a surprising upset over Sean Penn and Bill Murray—both had been favored by the critics. Depp, however, did not even attend the awards ceremony.

The following Sunday, on February 29, Johnny and his girlfriend, Vanessa Paradis, joined many other celebrities for the Oscars ceremony at Hollywood's Kodak Theatre. He would later say that his thoughts at that time were focused on one thing. He kept thinking the whole time, "Please, don't let me win."

And Johnny didn't win. Sean Penn, nominated in the same category for his dramatic role in *Mystic River*, took home the cherished Oscar for Best Actor. "When I didn't win . . . I was ecstatic," said Depp later. "Absolutely ecstatic. I applauded the lucky winner and said, 'Thank God!'"

Content in his defeat, Depp had, in fact, launched a new phase of his career. He had become the "Oscar-nominated Johnny Depp." And that decorative adjective now attached to his name could—and would—only get more impressive. Depp was now a Hollywood brand name. And he had proved that he could have commercial success without compromising his artistic integrity.

CHAPTER TWO

A DREAM OF A NIGHTMARE

Johnny Depp's early years were marked by frequent moves and money troubles. Born John Christopher Depp II on June 9, 1963, in Owensboro, Kentucky, he was the youngest of four children. His father, John Christopher Depp, was a civil engineer, and his mother, Betty Sue, worked as a waitress.

Because his father was called John, the son received the nickname Johnny. That name would stick throughout Johnny Depp's life. With his diverse heritage of German, Irish, French, and Cherokee ancestry, Johnny would grow up to become a young man with striking good looks.

As a young boy living in Kentucky, Johnny was very close to his maternal grandfather, whom he called PawPaw. Johnny spent a lot of time with his grandfather, but PawPaw died when Johnny was seven years old. Soon afterward, the Depps moved from Kentucky and settled in the southeastern Florida town of Miramar. There, Johnny's father became the town's director of public works.

A Rough Childhood

In Florida, the Depp family moved from place to place and struggled financially. At one time, they lived in a motel for about a

Today, Johnny is very close with his mother, Betty Sue Depp, shown here with her son. She often attends his premieres and walks down the red carpet with him. In fact, the two are so close that Johnny built her a home right next door to his Hollywood Hills home.

year. Johnny and his siblings—brother Danny and sisters Christine and Deborah—were continuously uprooted.

But even more troublesome, Johnny has said, was growing up in a household in which there was constant tension between his parents. From a young age, he was aware of their fighting, and it had a negative impact on him. "When I was growing up, I didn't have a very healthy family life," he explained in an interview. "We were about as messed up as you could get. I always swore to myself that if I ever had children of my own, I would do things right."

The family troubles were only part of Johnny's problems. He was also insecure about himself. In talking about his childhood with one reporter, he said, "I always felt like a total freak. I had the feeling of wanting to be accepted but not knowing how to go about being accepted as who I am."

Johnny's troubled childhood led to rebellious and at-risk behavior as a teen. He started smoking at age 12 and doing drugs at age 14. In a 1993 interview in *Details* magazine, he admitted that the stress of problems at home and his own insecurity led him to intentionally cut himself. Some scars on his arms remain today. In the *Details* interview, he explained his self-inflicted injuries, as well as the tattoos he wears:

> My body is a journal in a way. It's like what sailors used to do, where every tattoo meant something, a specific time in your life when you make a mark on yourself, whether you do it to yourself with a knife or with a professional tattoo artist.

Escape into Music

Music offered Johnny a way to escape from his problems. He told a *Rolling Stone* reporter that his uncle had inspired him to pick up the guitar:

> My mom and my dad weren't particularly musical.
> . . . But I did have an uncle who was a preacher,
> and he played hillbilly bluegrass guitar. . . . That

was where I got the bug: watching my uncle play the guitar with his little gospel group, right in front of me.

Around the age of 12, Johnny convinced his mother to buy him his first guitar. It was a $25 Decca electric guitar. He taught himself how to play using a book of guitar chords and from listening to records.

Before long, Johnny was spending a considerable amount of his time playing as part of a garage band. He told *Rolling Stone:*

> When I was about thirteen, I got together with some other kids in the neighborhood. This one guy had a bass, we knew a guy who had a PA system, we made our own lights. It was really ramshackle and great. We'd play at people's backyard parties. Everything from the Beatles to Led Zeppelin to Cheap Trick to Devo.

They called their rock band the Flame.

Johnny was 15 years old and the only kid still living at home when his parents divorced. Playing guitar became more important to him than anything else, including school. In addition to being a poor student while in high school, Johnny was known for getting into trouble. His fighting, drinking, smoking, shoplifting, and drug-taking got him suspended from school a number of times.

The Kids

In 1979, when Johnny was 16, he became the lead guitarist for a rock band called the Kids. Soon after, he dropped out of school to focus on music. He later explained: "When I left high school,

In the early 1980s Johnny was lead guitarist for a rock band called the Kids. This January 2007 photo shows him (center) reunited with the members of his old band at a charity benefit held in Pompano Beach, Florida.

I really didn't know what I wanted to do. The only thing that saved me was my band."

The Kids toured the Florida nightclub circuit, performing at gigs that earned him about $25 a night. The Kids had some success, obtaining jobs as opening acts for such punk rock heavyweights as Iggy Pop, the Ramones, Billy Idol, the Pretenders, and the Talking Heads.

Move to LA

In November 1983 the Kids decided to try to get a record deal. The best way to do that, the band members thought, was to head west. Johnny was in his junior year when he quit school, and he and his band moved to Los Angeles. To better fit into the LA scene, the band changed its name to Six Gun Method.

The following month Depp made a sudden commitment. In December 1983 he married his band's drummer's sister, Lori Anne Allison. Five years older than Johnny, Lori was also a musician. Years later he discussed his decision: "I was married when I was twenty. It was a strong bond with someone but I can't necessarily say I was in love. That's something that comes around once . . . maybe twice if you're lucky."

There was plenty of competition from other bands in LA, and the band members had to take side jobs to make any money. Johnny and Lori struggled to pay their bills. She found a job in the movie industry working as a makeup artist. He took on a variety of odd jobs such as selling T-shirts or working as a telemarketer selling personalized ballpoint pens over the phone. He also decided to try to make some money by getting an acting job.

On Elm Street

Depp got his start in acting with a little help from his friend, Nicolas Cage. Cage was already an established actor, having appeared in such films as *Valley Girl* (1983) and *Rumble Fish* (1983). Johnny had been introduced to the young actor by Lori, who did his makeup. Cage had quickly become a fan of Johnny's band.

Nicolas introduced Johnny to his agent, who got the aspiring actor an audition for a part in a horror flick. Wes Craven was casting the film *A Nightmare on Elm Street*. It was the first in what would become a series of successful *Nightmare* films.

Craven would later say that he had been influenced by his daughter when he chose Johnny for a major role in the movie.

READ MORE

A year younger than Depp, Nicolas Cage helped Johnny get his start. To learn more about the actor who went on to make blockbusters of his own, turn to page 48.

She had read lines with Johnny during the audition and had been impressed with his good looks.

Depp landed the role of Glen Lantz, the boyfriend of the film's heroine, Nancy. Johnny's character is asked to make sure she doesn't fall asleep. If she sleeps, Nancy would become the victim of the murderous Freddie Krueger, the ghost of a serial child murderer who haunts the nightmares of teenagers. Ultimately, Glen fails at keeping Nancy awake, which nearly causes her death. She survives, but Depp's character suffers a terrible fate. He falls victim to Krueger, and ends up sucked into a bed and then spat out in a bloody gush.

After the filming of *Nightmare* ended, Johnny became serious about his new career. To improve his skills, he enrolled in the Loft Studio, an acting school in Los Angeles. While his first movie character may have ended up dead, Depp's film career was now very much alive.

Freddy Krueger, the villain of the 1984 film *A Nightmare on Elm Street*, which was directed by Wes Craven. Critics touted Johnny Depp's first movie as highly imaginative and one of the most terrifying horror films of the 1980s.

CHAPTER THREE

AN UNWILLING TV STAR

Ending up dead in a teen horror thriller may not be the best way to launch a serious acting career. But it worked for Johnny. Following the November 1984 release of *A Nightmare on Elm Street*, he was looking at acting as a career, not just as a side job to make money. His band had broken up the previous summer, and its members had gone their separate ways.

The aspiring actor managed to get starring roles in two 1985 films—the campy teen sex comedy *Private Resort* and the cable television crime thriller *Slow Burn*. However, neither movie won him critical acclaim or success. In 1985 his personal life was also in trouble. Johnny and Lori decided to end their two-year-old marriage.

A New Opportunity

The following year, it looked like Johnny's career was on the rise when he landed a small part in a major movie by Oliver Stone. In addition to being an Oscar-winning screenwriter, Stone was also a talented director. He added Depp to the cast of his Vietnam War film *Platoon*.

Depp got the role of a private called Gator Lerner. His character speaks Vietnamese and serves as a translator for his unit.

Before filming began, cast members spent six months in the Philippines. There, they went through boot camp and basic combat training—just like real soldiers. Along with 30 other actors, Depp lived every aspect of an infantryman's life, from lugging gear to digging foxholes.

However, in the final version of the film, most of Depp's work playing Gator Lerner ended up being cut from the movie. Stone has explained his editing of *Platoon*:

I cut most of the Lerner role out of the film out of necessity. This character that looked like an average American kid but who could communicate effectively with the enemy in their own language—in the scenes Lerner was in he became a focus, he was a compelling character and Depp played him as such, I ran into the problem in editing that this Lerner character ended up being more interesting than the lead character of Chris Taylor [Charlie Sheen], which would throw the scenes and effectively the entire movie out of whack if I didn't trim them down.

In interviews, Depp has called the 1986 movie *Platoon* the first

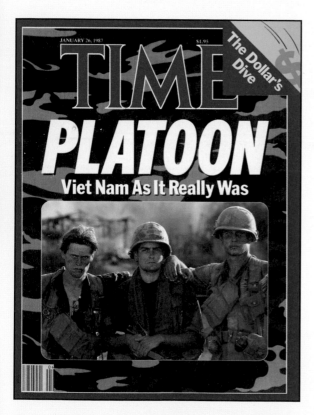

Time magazine features the three stars of *Platoon*, from left to right, Willem Dafoe, Charlie Sheen, and Tom Berenger. Most of Johnny's part was cut from the 1986 film.

"proper film" he appeared in. The drama gave moviegoers some insight into combat during the Vietnam War. It would go on to receive eight Academy Award nominations and win four Oscars, including Best Picture and Best Director. It would not be until 2006 that people would have the opportunity to see Depp's work in *Platoon*. Two decades after the film's initial release, Depp's scenes would be restored and included on the Twentieth Anniversary Collector's Edition DVD of *Platoon*.

But in 1986, Johnny was trying to decide what to do after *Platoon*. Once more, he turned to music as an outlet. He had met up with a band called the Rock City Angels, whose members had relocated from Miami to Los Angeles. They were looking for a guitarist, and Depp was interested. But the acting world wasn't ready to let him go just yet.

A Reluctant Undercover Cop

Initially, Johnny wanted nothing to do with acting on "the small screen," or television. He had started out getting roles in movies—on the "big screen"—and wanted to continue with working in film.

Then Johnny was offered the lead in a Fox TV series. The new program, called *21 Jump Street*, was based on a real-life operation in which young-looking members of the police force worked undercover in high schools. Refusing to even read the script, Depp declined the offer.

When the actor hired for the show did not work out, the *21 Jump Street* producers approached Johnny again. After telling himself that the series would probably only

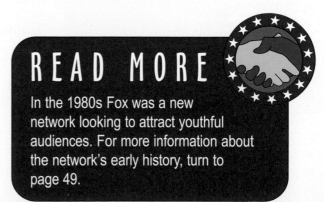

READ MORE

In the 1980s Fox was a new network looking to attract youthful audiences. For more information about the network's early history, turn to page 49.

run one season, he relented, and signed on to play Officer Tom Hanson. From the beginning, Johnny had mixed feelings about his character. "Hanson is not someone I'd want to have pizza with," he told one interviewer. "I don't believe in having undercover cops in high school—it's spying. The only thing I have in common with Tom Hanson is that we look alike."

But Johnny had no other work at the time. And television work was better than no work. The $45,000-per-episode salary he would eventually earn was also a factor in his decision to jump to the small screen.

By the time the pilot episode debuted on Fox on April 12, 1987, the network's publicity machine was marketing Depp's good looks and potential as a teen sensation. It was hoped that he would help win over the show's target audience, which consisted primarily of teenage girls.

Johnny got plenty of attention thanks to *21 Jump Street*'s success. His face was plastered all over teen fan magazines and thousands of fans wrote letters to him each week.

In 1987 Johnny was also thriving personally. Before landing the series, he had begun dating actress Sherilyn Fenn. She would also find fame on television later, starring in David Lynch's eerie and offbeat 1990–91 series *Twin Peaks*. However, since *21 Jump Street* was filmed in Vancouver, Canada, their relationship was strained by long separations.

An American Teen Idol

With the April 1987 launch of *21 Jump Street*, Johnny Depp suddenly became a teenage idol. Photographs and articles about the hot new star appeared in fan magazines. And viewer mail, much of it aimed directly at Depp, poured in. By the show's second season more than 10,000 letters a month would find their way to Johnny.

Each week the program addressed a range of issues related to juvenile crime. There were episodes on car thefts, burglaries, drug abuse, pregnancy, and peer pressure. Depp and other cast members recorded a series of public-service announcements that ran after certain episodes. The announcements, tackling such topics as AIDS and child abuse, were related to a specific program's storyline.

Actress Sherilyn Fenn and Johnny met in 1985 and dated for several years. During that time, she appeared in an episode of *21 Jump Street*.

Stuck on Jump Street

Despite his popularity Johnny was irritated with his new status as a teen idol. He was also concerned about the show's effect on his career as a serious actor. Although his agent, Tracey Jacobs, was receiving numerous film offers for him, the scripts featured roles that were all too similar to his character on *21 Jump Street*. Johnny feared the success of the series was pigeonholing him as Tom Hanson. And it did not help that the press continuously focused on his looks rather than his acting ability.

By the end of the second season Johnny was seriously trying to end his contract. And he was quoted as promising that after his contract on the series expired, he would only appear in films that he felt were right for him.

Still, Depp did not completely regret taking the role on *21 Jump Street*. He was able to see some benefits of the show and what he learned from it. Years later he shared those thoughts with a reporter from *The New York Times*:

> The series was great training, to work in front of a camera five days a week for four years. And it seems to have put me on the map, put me in a position to do things I really wanted to do. . . . But it was never anything morally I felt comfortable with. I mean, the idea of cops in high school is a scary thought.

Broken Engagements

Off the screen, Depp's romantic life was filled with turmoil. He had gotten engaged to actress Sherilyn Fenn. The couple, however, ended up spending a lot time apart as she pursued her acting career in Los Angeles and Johnny filmed *21 Jump Street* in Vancouver. They eventually had enough of the long-distance pressures, and the two ended their relationship in 1988.

Soon thereafter, Johnny began dating actress Jennifer Grey, who was most famous for her role in the 1987 popular film *Dirty Dancing*. They too became engaged. But their romance, which was also essentially a long-distance one, ended after eight months.

Meanwhile Depp also wanted to end another relationship—his contract with *21 Jump Street*. Eager to break away from his teen idol image, Depp continued to plead with his agent, Tracey Jacobs, to get him out of his contract. In 1989 Depp was letting some of his irritation show during interviews and making negative comments about his character and the entire show in general. The tabloids and gossip columns reported that he threw temper tantrums on the set and made outrageous demands. However, Johnny denied the stories, saying he was simply speaking his mind.

CHAPTER FOUR

BACK ON THE BIG SCREEN

Johnny finally heard from a film director offering a role that didn't feature him as a teenage heartthrob. Director John Waters, who was known for his offbeat and unusual films, wanted Depp to star in his latest project, a musical spoof called *Cry-Baby*.

Depp called Waters to discuss the offer. When Johnny expressed his dissatisfaction with being as a teen idol, Waters had a suggestion for him. He said that the best way to get rid of an unwanted image might be to make fun of it. And Johnny could accomplish that by starring in his movie.

Lip-synching

Waters sent Johnny a script. Soon afterward *Cry-Baby*, a musical parody of Elvis Presley movies, became Depp's next project. The film is set in Baltimore in 1954, during the beginning of the rock-and-roll era. Depp starred as Wade "Cry-Baby" Walker, a grief-stricken, misunderstood Baltimore juvenile delinquent from the wrong

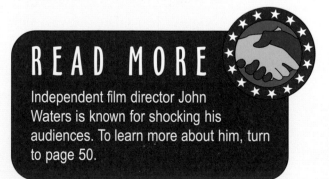

READ MORE

Independent film director John Waters is known for shocking his audiences. To learn more about him, turn to page 50.

side of the tracks. His nickname Cry-Baby comes from the perpetual tear in his eye—he is grieving over the loss of his parents, who have both been killed in the electric chair.

The filming of *Cry-Baby* was a collaborative process: Depp took direction from Waters during rehearsals, while he offered his own creative ideas about his role. With his musical background, Depp was also able to suggest instruments and equipment to use in the musical portions of the film. But when it came to the film's campy musical numbers, he lip-synched his songs instead of providing the vocals.

Released in April 1990, *Cry-Baby* helped change how people viewed Depp. Once seen as a one-dimensional television actor, he was now seen as capable of much more. Depp returned to *21 Jump Street* after shooting for *Cry-Baby* finished. However, he had finally been able to renegotiate his contractual obligations. Johnny only needed to complete the 1989–90 season before he could return to the big screen full-time. He was released from his contract after *Jump Street*'s fourth season.

Love at First Sight

In June 1989, Depp attended the New York premiere of *Great Balls of Fire*, the biographical drama about rock-and-roll legend Jerry Lee Lewis. One of the film's stars was Winona Ryder. She played Myra Gale Brown, the singer's teenage bride. At the premiere Johnny, now 27, and 17-year-old Winona met at the concession stand. The attraction was immediate and mutual.

Despite the more than nine-year age difference, Johnny and Winona started dating. It was just five months later that they announced

READ MORE

To learn more about the career of actress Winona Ryder, turn to page 51.

Johnny holds Winona Ryder's hand at the premiere of *Cry-Baby* in 1990. Johnny and Winona were Hollywood's "it" couple for the duration of their relationship, and the paparazzi followed them everywhere.

their engagement. From that point on, the paparazzi followed the couple everywhere.

The Lonely Little Kid Inside

In 1990, Depp's career took another interesting turn. He starred opposite Ryder in director Tim Burton's fractured fairy tale *Edward Scissorhands*. Ryder and Burton had already worked together on the popular, as well as dark and quirky,

READ MORE

For more information on director, producer, and screenwriter Tim Burton, and Johnny's long association with him, turn to page 52.

comedy *Beetlejuice*. Despite the competition among several Hollywood big names for the lead role of Edward Scissorhands, Burton decided to take a chance on Depp. The director cast Ryder as the female lead, hoping that the off-screen romance of Johnny and Winona would enrich their onscreen relationship.

Edward Scissorhands is a fanciful modern-day fable about an inventor's humanlike creation. The title character is an innocent, soulful lad with scissors instead of hands, because his creator died before he could give Edward hands. The unusual character seemed a stretch for Depp. But the more he thought about the role, the more familiar it became. He explained how he felt about it in an interview:

> It wasn't similar to anything I'd played before, to put it mildly. I thought, "No way that people would see me as Edward." Then I realized that Edward was all alone, and inside of all of us is this lonely little kid. Edward is a total outsider. I really know how that feels.

The bladed scissor hands used in the film *Edward Scissorhands* are displayed in front of a movie publicity shot autographed by stars Johnny Depp and Winona Ryder.

Years later *Entertainment Weekly* would note that Burton rescued Depp from his status as "reluctant heartthrob" by casting him in *Edward Scissorhands*. Johnny's good looks played no part in the story. As *EW* noted, the role called for "covering his face with scars and Kabuki makeup to play a fragile outcast." Johnny would play this kind of character—the outcast—again and again in the years to come.

Released in December 1990, *Edward Scissorhands* earned more than $50 million in the United States alone. It also brought Depp some critical notice as well as a Golden Globe nomination as Best Actor. Now he could say an official good-bye to the small screen and his teen idol image.

Johnny had enjoyed playing the oddball loner role. He admitted in an interview with *The New York Times* that he had developed a close bond with his film character:

> I hope this won't sound completely corny, but I loved playing Edward so much, because there is nothing cynical or jaded or impure about him, nothing mean about him. It's almost a letdown to look in the mirror and realize I'm not Edward. I really miss him.

A Productive Stretch

Depp soon started a highly productive phase in his career. Over the next decade, he tackled a variety of projects. And he began to live up to his tremendous potential as an actor.

In 1993 Johnny had several critical successes. Starring opposite Mary Stuart Masterson, he made a showy turn as a gifted, but eccentric, mime in the offbeat romantic fable *Benny and Joon*. As part of the film, Johnny performed his own renditions of the classic routines of silent-era comic geniuses Buster

Keaton, Charlie Chaplin, and Harold Lloyd. These comic legends were as popular with Depp as they were with his character. In addition to being able to pay tribute to his idols, he was also able to show audiences that he too was a gifted and graceful modern-day clown. His performance in *Benny and Joon* also brought him a second Golden Globe nod.

Later that year Depp gave a convincing performance as a young man torn between living his own life and caring for his family in *What's Eating Gilbert Grape*. The whimsical comedy-drama also starred another actor on the rise, Leonardo DiCaprio. In his role as Gilbert's mentally disabled little brother, Arnie, DiCaprio netted an Oscar nomination.

Johnny again teamed with director Tim Burton in *Ed Wood*, a fictionalized biopic of an eccentric director who worked during the 1950s. Burton has often described Depp as a "great character

From left to right, Johnny Depp, Leonardo DiCaprio, and Juliette Lewis appear in a scene from the 1993 film *What's Eating Gilbert Grape*.

actor in a leading man's body," which made him perfect for this new project. Interested in playing demanding characters, Johnny turned down roles in potential blockbusters to star in *Ed Wood*. Among the higher-profile films he rejected parts in were *Speed*, *Interview with the Vampire*, and *Indecent Proposal*.

Ed Wood is a very good director's very good movie about a very bad director. The film's title character is a real-life moviemaker generally regarded as the worst director in movie history. Johnny took on the role of the obsessive, cross-dressing Ed Wood in this poetic black-and-white tribute. Veteran actor Martin Landau, who costarred in *Ed Wood*, would earn a Best Supporting Actor Oscar for his work in the film. He played opposite Johnny as actor Bela Lugosi, the star of Woods' movie *Plan 9 from Outer Space*.

Struggling with Celebrity

While Johnny was cementing his reputation as a major movie actor, his tabloid profile was also rising. Newspapers and celebrity magazines chronicled his off-screen exploits with more and more frequency. They noted how in 1993 Johnny Depp became part-owner of the Viper Room, a nightclub on West Hollywood's Sunset Strip. The place was the site where the young actor River Phoenix died of a drug overdose that October. A year later, Depp would end his connection to the club.

Meanwhile, Johnny's relationship with Winona Ryder was falling apart. Both of their screen careers were thriving, and they were often separated. The couple was also hounded by the press, which irritated Johnny. In one interview, he discussed the difficulty of being a celebrity and constantly under scrutiny by the media:

Hollywood's famous nightclub the Viper Room. Traditionally known as a hotspot for Hollywood's young up-and-coming stars, the nightclub was partially owned by Johnny during the early 1990s.

> For a few years there I was ready to jump out of my skin—and that feeling comes back every now and again. The idea that your private life is displayed before the public and kind of dissected and a lot of fiction gets written about you is a drag—a real drag. But it's something you just have to deal with. How do I deal with it? I don't read anything.

The Depp-Ryder relationship ended in 1993, leaving Johnny with a "Winona Forever" tattoo on his arm. He later had the tattoo partially removed, editing it so it read "Wino Forever."

In 1994 Johnny went public with an announcement about his new relationship with British supermodel Kate Moss. But love did little to calm Depp's sometimes wild off-screen ways. In September Moss was staying with him in the Mark Hotel in New York City while Johnny was on a publicity tour for *Ed Wood*.

During their stay, the police were summoned because of a reported disturbance in his room. When they got there, they discovered that the room had been trashed.

Johnny was arrested. He was released the next afternoon after agreeing to pay more than $9,000 in damages. Depp would later admit to having problems during the early and mid-1990s with drinking. He once recalled, "That was kind of a nasty, darker period for me. I can't say I was completely unhappy, but I couldn't get a grasp on it, so I spent years poisoning myself."

Following His Own Path

Much more adept at managing his career than his reputation, Johnny continued down the movie road less traveled by playing another romantic misfit. In the compelling *Don Juan DeMarco*, released in April 1995, he costarred with acting icon Marlon Brando. Johnny played a suicidal psychiatric patient who claims to be legendary lover Don Juan. Brando appears as his psychiatrist. Critics described Depp as inspired in his role of a tenderly romantic mental patient who casts a spell with deadpan sincerity.

Johnny was not able to maintain that high level of acting as he moved through his next few projects released that year. He appeared in the western *Dead Man*, directed by Jim Jarmusch, and the

After his 1993 breakup with Winona Ryder, Johnny dated British model Kate Moss. The combination of her wild ways and his partying lifestyle continued to get him in trouble, and their relationship did not last long.

political thriller *Nick of Time*. Neither film made much of an impact on reviewers or moviegoers. Two years later, Depp redeemed himself with *Donnie Brasco*. The gripping 1997 undercover crime drama was well received and gave him a chance to work with famed actor Al Pacino.

In 1998, Depp made his debut behind the camera with the poorly received western drama, *The Brave*. He directed himself and Marlon Brando in a story about Native Americans and the cycle of poverty. It was the first time that Depp took a seat in the director's chair for a feature film.

In making his directorial debut, Johnny Depp continued to follow his own path. He chose to pursue what interested him, not wanting to be pushed in any direction by the quest for stardom and big box-office sales. In November 1999 he told *Entertainment Weekly*:

> Maybe I'm a dummy, but I don't worry that a lot of my films haven't had big results at the box office, because I'm not a businessman. Believe me, I would love for one of my movies to be accepted by a wide audience, but I'm not going to do a film just because it's going to do that.

CHAPTER FIVE

WALKING THE GANGPLANK TO SUPERSTARDOM

After the chilly reception of his directorial debut *The Brave*, Johnny went back in front of the cameras. For his next role, he played real-life gonzo journalist—and friend—Hunter S. Thompson in director Terry Gilliam's 1998 film *Fear and Loathing in Las Vegas*. The movie is based on Thompson's book by the same title. It follows the oddball journalist's adventures in Las Vegas. The story takes place during the late 1960s, in the midst of America's drug culture.

Box-Office Slump

In an interview with the *New York Daily News*, Gilliam raved about Depp's performance in *Fear and Loathing in Las Vegas*. The director noted:

Johnny Depp and Hunter S. Thompson at the New York City premiere of *Fear and Loathing in Las Vegas*, held in May 1998.

Johnny enjoys losing himself in a character,

and every character he's played is totally believable, no matter how bizarre it is. Once he's in there, he's in there 100%, wherever it leads. If it's truthful, he goes for it. He totally became Hunter Thompson.

However, the story of Hunter Thompson did not appeal to critics or movie audiences. In the summer of 2008, Johnny would narrate a documentary on Thompson. Entitled *Gonzo: The Life and Work of Dr. Hunter S. Thompson*, the documentary would be more favorably received by the critics than Gilliam's 1998 film was.

Johnny's box-office slump continued in 1999. He headlined director Roman Polanski's tepid supernatural thriller *The Ninth Gate*. Depp also costarred with Charlize Theron in the forgettable science fiction film *The Astronaut's Wife*. The latter movie would earn him his biggest salary ever ($8 million), but the film itself would bomb.

Living for Family

Personally, Johnny was on an upswing. In 1998, he had begun a new relationship with French singer and actress Vanessa Paradis. The two met in Paris, France, that summer, while Depp was filming *The Ninth Gate*. In May 1999, Johnny and Vanessa had become proud parents of a daughter named Lily-Rose Melody Depp. In an interview, Johnny expressed his feelings about fatherhood:

READ MORE

Vanessa Paradis was a successful singer long before she met Johnny. To learn more about her many accomplishments, turn to page 53.

As of May 27, 1999, at 8:25 P.M. my life changed . . . . Everything became clear. I had been walking around for 36 years in a haze. . . . it wasn't until I connected up with Vanessa and we celebrated the birth of our daughter Lily-Rose that I felt that I really had something to live for. I knew why I had to be alive.

Back to Burton

In 1999 Johnny was again working with Tim Burton. In *Sleepy Hollow*, released in November of that year, Depp played Ichabod

Johnny and Vanessa share a laugh as he receives his star at the Hollywood Walk of Fame ceremony in November 1999.

Crane. Ichabod is the main character in Burton's kooky, spooky version of Washington Irving's gothic tale of the headless horseman. Christina Ricci played his love interest.

After finishing *Sleepy Hollow*, Johnny returned to Hollywood to receive his star on the Hollywood Walk of Fame. Located along Hollywood Boulevard and Vine Street, the star-studded sidewalk features the names of notable people in the entertainment industry. Director Tim Burton and actor Martin Landau attended the November 19, 1999, ceremony.

Depp would later confess that he found it ironic to have his name placed on the Walk of Fame. Nevertheless, he enjoyed receiving the honor, he told an interviewer:

I thought it was funny. There's something perverse that I like about it. Something absurd about it. I mean, a town that's never acknowledged my presence, really . . . Hollywood being a place that I've been at constant battle with for the last fifteen, sixteen years.

Johnny's Angels

Since the birth of his daughter in 1999, Johnny has become involved in a number of children's charities. One organization he has helped is the Children's Hospice and Palliative Care Coalition, based in Watsonville, California. The group provides support to families of children diagnosed with life-threatening conditions.

Johnny's charitable efforts have also inspired his fans. A group of them created Johnny's Angels: Depp Fans for Charity. On its Web site, the organization notes that its members work to find a "meaningful way for Depp fans to honor an actor whose talent and humanity have inspired so many." The group raises money for Children's Hospice and works to help families whose children have life-threatening and terminal illnesses.

From Gypsy to Inspector

Johnny has continued to work steadily on a range of films. Reuniting with Christina Ricci, he starred as a gypsy in the World War II drama *The Man Who Cried*, which was released in 2000. That same year he also took on two small roles. He appeared in *Before Night Falls*, a biopic about Cuban poet Reynaldo Arenas. And Depp played a gypsy again in *Chocolat*. In the French film, he appears as Roux, a wanderer who becomes involved with a woman who isn't afraid to go against convention in her small village.

In his next two projects, Johnny took on roles that represented both sides of the law. In *Blow*, released in 2001, he played a real-life drug kingpin. The same year he played an English police inspector on the track of famed serial killer Jack the Ripper in the film *From Hell*.

A Signature Role

But this string of projects merely served as prelude to what would become his splashiest signature role. The role of Captain Jack Sparrow would be the one that would finally make Johnny Depp a major marquee attraction and land him squarely on Hollywood's A-list of actors.

On April 9, 2002, Johnny and Vanessa welcomed their second child, John Christopher Depp III, nicknamed Jack. That same year, Depp accepted the role of Captain Jack Sparrow in *Pirates of the Caribbean: The Curse of the Black Pearl*. Some fans may have accused the well-respected actor of "selling out" artistically, by agreeing to appear in the likely blockbuster. After all,

Johnny and *Pirates* costar Orlando Bloom celebrate at the premiere of *The Curse of the Black Pearl* at Disneyland in 2003. (Inset) His Jack Sparrow role would have such an impact on Johnny that he would later tattoo the character's name on his forearm.

Pirates of the Caribbean, with its Disney theme-park ride origins, was a period piece with a built-in audience.

And the film *was* a blockbuster. Released in the summer of 2003—just after Johnny celebrated his 40th birthday—*Pirates of the Caribbean: The Curse of the Black Pearl* was an instant hit. Depp's portrayal of Captain Jack as a pirate with slurred speech and a glistening row of gold-capped teeth was central to the film's success.

More Roles, More Awards

After the first *Pirates* film, Johnny received his second Academy Award nomination for Best Actor. It recognized his performance in *Finding Neverland*, which was released in November 2004. He played Scottish author James Matthew Barrie, the writer of the beloved children's book *Peter Pan*, among others.

Teaming up again with Tim Burton, Johnny starred in two projects released in 2005. The first, *Charlie and the Chocolate*

Johnny signs autographs for eager fans at Grauman's Chinese Theater in Hollywood during the world premiere of *Charlie and the Chocolate Factory* in July 2005.

Factory was based on the Roald Dahl children's novel of the same name. Depp starred as offbeat candy factory owner Willy Wonka. A second Tim Burton project that year had him lend his voice to the animated adventure *Corpse Bride*. The former was a big hit. The latter was a respectable one.

The huge success of *Pirates of the Caribbean: The Curse of the Black Pearl* guaranteed that *Pirates* sequels would follow. Johnny signed on to appear twice more as Captain Jack Sparrow. The plan called for two sequels to be released in the summers of 2006 and 2007—one subtitled *Dead Man's Chest*, and the other, *At World's End*. The second and third entries in the *Pirates* trilogy were to be shot back-to-back in the Bahamas.

Even with this busy schedule, Johnny's life was not consumed only with acting. In October 2006, he received the Courage to

The *Pirates* franchise was such an overwhelming success that in 2006 Disney modified its classic theme park attraction to incorporate an animatronic figure of Captain Jack Sparrow. Here, Johnny poses next to his character inside the ride.

Care Award in recognition of his work with Children's Hospital Los Angeles. This facility devotes itself to providing critically ill children with medical care regardless of their families' ability to pay.

While critics may not have loved the two *Pirates* sequels, moviegoers flocked to theaters to see them. Released in July 2006, *Pirates of the Caribbean: Dead Man's Chest* broke several records. At the time, it commanded the highest opening-day gross and the highest opening-weekend gross. "Crazy for Johnny, or Captain Jack?" asked *USA Today*, wondering aloud whether it was the actor or his fictional alter ego that was responsible for the movie's staggering opening weekend. The paper reported that *Pirates of the Caribbean: Dead Man's Chest* raked in $135.6 million at the box office in the first weekend. The film went on to earn more than $423 million, making it one of the highest-grossing films of all time.

A year later, in May 2007, *Pirates of the Caribbean: At World's End* also hit box-office gold. This meant that the entire *Pirates* trilogy came close to earning $3 billion worldwide.

The Demon Barber and Beyond

After his reign as the world's favorite pirate, Johnny reunited with Tim Burton yet again. Their sixth film together was the 2007 musical *Sweeney Todd: The Demon Barber of Fleet Street*. Filming stopped temporarily in May 2007, when Johnny and Vanessa's daughter, Lily-Rose, suffered kidney failure. She spent several days recovering in the Great Ormond Street Hospital, in London. In gratitude to the hospital for helping his daughter, Depp would later donate $2 million to the children's medical center. He also reportedly pledged another $20 million for hospital renovations.

Sweeney Todd is adapted from the Tony Award–winning 1979 Broadway musical by Stephen Sondheim. The fictional story, set in 1800s London is a unique combination of musical and violent

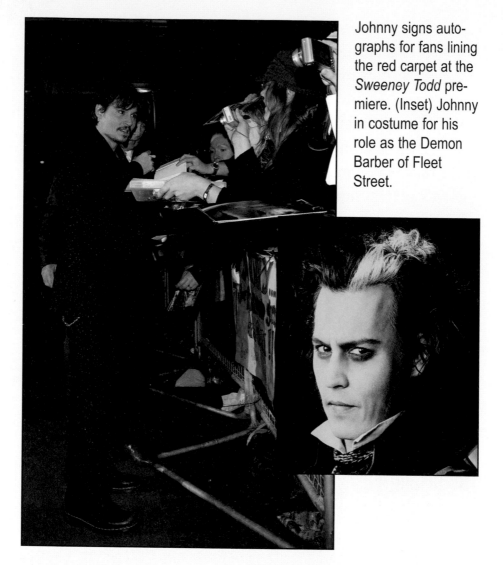

Johnny signs autographs for fans lining the red carpet at the *Sweeney Todd* premiere. (Inset) Johnny in costume for his role as the Demon Barber of Fleet Street.

thriller. A revenge-minded barber returns to London after years of being imprisoned on false charges. He sets up shop and begins killing off those who have wronged him. A widowed baker named Mrs. Lovett, played by Helena Bonham Carter, helps the murderer by turning his victims' remains into meat pies.

To the surprise and delight of Depp fans, Johnny sings his own songs in *Sweeney Todd*. His performance and the film itself received mostly positive reviews. Depp won the Golden Globe for Best Performance by an Actor in a Motion Picture, Musical or Comedy, for his work. The film also brought him his third Academy Award nomination.

While Johnny did not win the Oscar, many of his fans believe it is only a matter of time before he finally brings home this honor. Awards, however, are not what motivate him. As for the future, fans and critics alike have learned to expect the unexpected from this uniquely talented actor. One thing is guaranteed, however. Johnny Depp will continue to seek out interesting and unusual parts to play.

With his talent for skillfully portraying iconic characters in films, Johnny Depp has firmly secured his place in Hollywood history.

American Film's Biggest Award

The Oscars are annual awards presented by the Academy of Motion Picture Arts and Sciences. Members of the Academy vote by specific categories identifying the best artists, performers, and technicians who have done the best film work over the previous calendar year.

The winner receives a 13-1/2-inch-tall golden statuette called the Oscar. Each figurine shows a man holding a sword and standing on a reel of film. The name *Oscar* dates from 1931, according to legend. At that time, the Academy librarian is said to have exclaimed that the statuette looked like her Uncle Oscar. The nickname wasn't officially used until 1939.

When the Academy Award ceremonies were first held in 1929, the awards represented a way of rewarding fine work and bringing respect and attention to the movie industry. During the early years, the awards were presented at small banquets in various Hollywood hotels. By the mid-1940s, the Award ceremonies were held at a series of Los Angeles theaters and auditoriums, including Grauman's Chinese Theatre and the Shrine Auditorium. Today, they are held in the Kodak Theatre in Hollywood and are telecast to a huge international audience. The original Academy had just 36 members, whereas today there are more than 6,500 members and voters.

The Oscar statuette has largely remained the same since the first Academy Awards ceremony in 1929.

Pepé Le Pew

Johnny has said that he borrowed certain mannerisms for his Captain Jack Sparrow character from a cartoon skunk named Pepé Le Pew. The cartoon character combined the traits of a perfect gentleman, a great lover, and a hopeless romantic. He often appeared in fruitless pursuit of "the love of his life." Pepé Le Pew had been brought to life in the 1940s by animator Chuck Jones.

The origins of Pepé can be traced to several sources. Some people say he was based on a character named Pepé le Moko, played by French actor Charles Boyer in the film *Algiers*. That movie was itself a remake of the French film *Pepé Le Moko*. Others have claimed that the character was actually based on another French actor named Maurice Chevalier.

Voiced by Mel Blanc, who worked on many Warner Bros. cartoons, Pepé Le Pew first appeared in 1945 in a cartoon entitled *The Odor-able Kitty*. The skunk went on to become a regular character in the Looney Tunes and Merrie Melodies cartoon series produced by the Warner Bros. Studio's animation division. In 1949, the Pepé Le Pew cartoon *For Scent-Imental Reasons* won the Oscar for Best Short Subject.

Animator Chuck Jones, the man responsible for creating Pepé Le Pew as part of the Looney Tunes cartoon series.

Nicolas Cage

Nicolas Cage was born Nicolas Kim Coppola on January 7, 1964, in Long Beach California. He changed his name early on in his career in hopes of carving out a reputation separate from that of his famous uncle, director Francis Ford Coppola.

Cage's first film role was a bit part in *Fast Times at Ridgemont High*, in 1982. But it was his first leading role in *Valley Girl*, released the following year, that truly launched his career. During the 1980s Nicolas Cage appeared in such films as *Birdy, Peggy Sue Got Married, Raising Arizona*, and *Moonstruck*. The early 1990s saw *Wild at Heart* and *Honeymoon in Vegas*. But it was his fierce, critically acclaimed portrayal of an alcoholic screenwriter who sets out to drink himself to death in 1995's *Leaving Las Vegas* that brought him the Oscar for Best Actor in a Leading Role and made him one of the biggest stars in the movie business. He was later nominated for another Best Actor Oscar in the 2002 film *Adaptation*.

Among the actor's most commercially successful films are those in which Cage plays an action hero. They include *The Rock* (1996), *National Treasure* (2004), and *National Treasure: Book of Secrets* (2007). Cage has also worked as a director and producer through his production company Saturn Films.

Nicolas Cage smiles as he holds his Oscar for Best Actor in the 1995 film *Leaving Las Vegas*.

The Fourth Network

For years, there were three major television networks: ABC, CBS, and NBC. The Fox Broadcasting Company—named after its sister movie company, 20th Century Fox—launched on October 9, 1986. At that time it broadcast to 96 stations.

The network was still a fledgling enterprise when its hour-long police drama series, *21 Jump Street*, premiered in 1987. At the time, the new network was trying to hold its own as it competed for ratings against the three larger, more established networks. It was to be an uphill climb for the network, which is part of the Fox Entertainment Group. The Fox Entertainment Group is also a division of the News Corporation, a company run by Australian global media tycoon Rupert Murdoch.

While the new fourth network had a big corporation behind it, it faced many challenges since it had fewer stations than its Big Three competitors. They each had more than 200 affiliates.

Fox tried to carve out its own niche by portraying itself as edgy and youth-oriented. And *21 Jump Street* definitely attracted a youthful audience. Other early Fox offerings included *Married with Children*, *The Tracey Ullman Show*, *The Simpsons*, *America's Most Wanted*, and *COPS*.

The Fox Broadcasting Company was still new when *21 Jump Street* first aired in 1987. By the mid-1990s it had established itself as a major fourth network in the broadcasting industry.

The Unpredictable John Waters

For many decades John Waters, born April 27, 1946, has been an independent director of offbeat, often outrageous, movies. Most of his work celebrates his native Baltimore. But his films also tend to poke fun at mainstream audiences' sensibilities.

Early in his career, Waters was intentionally offensive. The films that he directed, wrote, and produced contained all sorts of disturbing subject matter. They included *Mondo Trasho* (1969), *Pink Flamingos* (1972), and *Female Trouble* (1974). Waters' films played mostly on the cult art-house circuit, often at midnight screenings.

In the late 1980s Waters made a move in the direction of mainstream cinema with *Hairspray* (1988). His subsequent directorial outings continued to demonstrate his playful sense of humor and desire to shock. Among them are *Serial Mom* (1994), *Cecil B. Demented* (2000), and *A Dirty Shame* (2004). But as his moviemaking skills grew, so did the size of his audiences and the reach of his films.

In recent years, Waters has found broader acceptance for his work. *Hairspray* was turned into a Tony Award–winning Broadway musical in 2002. The play was then adapted in 2007 into a movie musical. Waters' musical *Cry-Baby*, which opened on Broadway in April 2008, was nominated for four Tony Awards.

Renowned for his many campy and outrageous films, independent director John Waters "went mainstream" in his 1990 parody film *Cry-Baby*, which featured Johnny Depp in the lead as a rock-and-roll musician and teen rebel.

Actress
Winona Ryder

Born October 29, 1971, Winona Laura Horowitz was named for the town of her birth: Winona, Minnesota. When she was 10 years old, her family moved to Petaluma, California. Soon afterward she was taking acting lessons at the American Conservatory Theater, in nearby San Francisco.

Winona got her first role in the 1986 comedy-drama *Lucas*. At that time she changed her name to Winona Ryder. It was only after being cast as the troubled teen in Tim Burton's 1988 *Beetlejuice* that she came to the attention of the public. She appeared next as a murderess in *Heathers* (1989). Despite the negative role, Winona established the character in a sympathetic way.

Some of Winona's most well-regarded roles include that of Wilhelmina "Mina" Murray in *Dracula* (1992), Jo in the film *Little Women* (1994), and Susanna Kaysen in *Girl, Interrupted* (1999). She won the Golden Globe Award for Best Supporting Actress for *Age of Innocence* (1993). That film also earned her a nomination for an Academy Award for Best Supporting Actress. In 1995 Ryder was nominated for an Oscar for Best Actress for *Little Women*.

Actress Winona Ryder. Five months after she and Johnny met, in June 1989, they were engaged. For the next four years, the celebrity couple carried on an intense relationship that suffered at times from incidents with the paparazzi and relentless media scrutiny. She and Johnny ultimately broke up in October 1993.

Director, Producer, and Screenwriter Tim Burton

Timothy William Burton has gained a reputation as a film director with an interest in the offbeat and quirky. Born August 25, 1958, in Burbank, California, Burton grew up with a love of drawing. After attending the California Institute of Arts, in Valencia, California, he went on to work in 1979 for Walt Disney Studies as an animator.

Burton soon left Disney to follow his own path. His first success came with the 1985 film *Pee-wee's Big Adventure*, starring comedian Paul Reubens. It was followed by the popular ghost fantasy and horror story *Beetlejuice*, released in 1988. By 1989 Burton had formed his own production company and directed the commercially successful *Batman*. The following year, he directed *Edward Scissorhands*, a film that helped Johnny Depp establish himself as an actor rather than a teen idol.

Burton has continued to make films the way he wanted to, writing and producing the stop motion animation musical *The Nightmare Before Christmas*. Released in 1993, the film was a commercial and critical success. Burton is also known for *Batman Returns* (1992), *Mars Attacks!* (1996), *Planet of the Apes* (2001), and *Big Fish* (2003). He directed Johnny Depp in *Ed Wood* (1994), which won Burton two Oscars. Depp also appeared in Burton's *Sleepy Hollow* (1999), *Charlie and the Chocolate Factory* (2005), and *Sweeney Todd* (2007). Depp is the godfather of Burton's son, Billy.

Tim Burton became close friends with Johnny Depp after working with him on *Edward Scissorhands*. That film was the first of many collaborations between the two.

Vanessa Paradis

Singer and actress Vanessa Chantal Paradis, was born December 22, 1972, in the Parisian suburb of St.-Maur-des-Fosses. She found fame as a singer when she was just eight years old when she appeared on the television show *L'Ecole des Fans*. By 1985, she had produced her first single. Her first hit, *Joe le Taxi*, came out two years later. It reached number one in France and number three in the United Kingdom the following year.

Vanessa was 16 years old when her first film was released. In 1989 her debut movie *Noce Blanche* won her the César Award (the national film award for France) for Most Promising Actress.

In 1992 Vanessa worked in the United States and produced an album along with rock musician Lenny Kravitz, her boyfriend at the time. She subsequently appeared in several films and as a model for Coco Chanel. Her 2000 album *Bliss* was dedicated to Johnny Depp and their daughter. Other albums include *M&J* (1988), *Vanessa Paradis* (1992), and *Divinidylle* (2007).

Johnny and Vanessa divide their time between their estate in Hollywood Hills, Los Angeles, and a villa in southern France. They also own an island in the Bahamas and apartments in Paris and New York City.

Vanessa Paradis was a successful actress and singer before she met Johnny Depp. Together she and Johnny have two children, Lily-Rose Melody and John "Jack" Christopher Depp.

Chronology

1963: John Christopher Depp II is born on June 9 in Owensboro, Kentucky. He is known by the nickname Johnny.

1971: The Depp family moves to Miramar, Florida.

1975: Johnny begins to learn how to play the guitar.

1978: Johnny's parents, Betty Sue and John Depp, divorce.

1979: Johnny drops out of high school to pursue a music career.

1983: Johnny moves to Los Angeles with his band, the Kids, which changes its name to Six Gun Method. He marries Lori Anne Allison.

1984: He debuts as a movie actor in the horror film *A Nightmare on Elm Street*.

1985: Lori and Johnny divorce.

1987: Johnny stars on the Fox television show *21 Jump Street*.

1988: Tracey Jacobs becomes Johnny's agent.

1990: Johnny stars in the John Waters film *Cry-Baby* and the Tim Burton film *Edward Scissorhands*.

1993: Johnny receives critical praise for his roles in *What's Eating Gilbert Grape* and *Benny and Joon*.

1994: He works again with Tim Burton in the biopic *Ed Wood*.

1995: Johnny appears in three films: *Don Juan DeMarco*, *Dead Man*, and *Nick of Time*.

1996: Johnny directs his first full-length film, *The Brave*.

1997: He costars with Al Pacino in *Donnie Brasco*.

1998: During the shooting of *The Ninth Gate* in Paris, Johnny meets and starts dating Vanessa Paradis. *Fear and Loathing in Las Vegas* is released.

1999: Johnny stars as Ichabod Crane in Tim Burton's *Sleepy Hollow*; Vanessa gives birth to their daughter, Lily-Rose Melody Depp, on May 27.

2000: Johnny appears in *Before Night Falls* and *Chocolat*.

2002: Vanessa Paradis gives birth to a son, John "Jack" Christopher Depp III, on April 9.

2003: The release of *Pirates of the Caribbean: The Curse of the Black Pearl* brings new acclaim to Johnny, who stars as Captain Jack Sparrow.

2004: Johnny receives his first Academy Award nomination, for Best Actor in *Pirates of the Caribbean: The Curse of the Black Pearl*. He stars as *Peter Pan* author J. M. Barrie in *Finding Neverland*.

2005: He stars as candy factory owner Willy Wonka in the Tim Burton film *Charlie and the Chocolate Factory*.

2006: Johnny reprises his role as Captain Jack in the sequel *Pirates of the Caribbean: Dead Man's Chest*.

2007: He appears as Captain Jack in the sequel *Pirates of the Caribbean: At World's End*; he also stars as the title character in Tim Burton's musical *Sweeney Todd*.

2008: Johnny wins the Golden Globe for Best Performance by an Actor for his role in *Sweeney Todd*.

Accomplishments/Awards
Filmography

A Nightmare on Elm Street
    (1984)
Private Resort (1985)
Slow Burn (1986)
Platoon (1986)
Cry-Baby (1990)
Edward Scissorhands (1990)
Freddy's Dead: The Final
    Nightmare (1991)
Arizona Dream (1991)
What's Eating Gilbert Grape?
    (1993)
Benny and Joon (1993)
Ed Wood (1994)
Don Juan DeMarco (1995)
Dead Man (1995)
Nick of Time (1995)
Donnie Brasco (1996)
The Brave (1996)
Cannes Man (1996)
LA Without a Map (1998)
Fear and Loathing in
    Las Vegas (1998)
The Astronaut's Wife (1999)
The Ninth Gate (1999)
Sleepy Hollow (1999)
The Man Who Cried (2000)
Before Night Falls (2000)

Chocolat (2000)
Blow (2001)
From Hell (2001)
Pirates of the Caribbean:
    The Curse of the Black
    Pearl (2003)
Once Upon a Time in Mexico
    (2003)
Finding Neverland (2004)
The Libertine (2004)
Secret Window (2004)
Happily Ever After
    (2004; French film)
Tim Burton's Corpse Bride
    (2005)
Charlie and the
    Chocolate Factory (2005)
Pirates of the Caribbean: Dead
    Man's Chest (2006)
Pirates of the Caribbean: At
    World's End (2007)
Sweeney Todd: The Demon
    Barber of Fleet Street (2007)
The Imaginarium of Doctor
    Parnassus (2009)
Public Enemies (2009)
Shantaram (2009)
The Rum Diary (2009)

Awards

Oscar for Best Actor in a Leading Role

2004 Nominated, *Pirates of the Caribbean: The Curse of the Black Pearl* (2003)

2005 Nominated, *Finding Neverland* (2004)

2008 Nominated, *Sweeney Todd: The Demon Barber of Fleet Street* (2007)

Golden Globe for Best Performance by an Actor in a Motion Picture—Comedy/Musical

1991 Nominated, *Edward Scissorhands* (1990)

1994 Nominated, *Benny and Joon* (1993)

1995 Nominated, *Ed Wood,* (1994)

2004 Nominated, *Pirates of the Caribbean: The Curse of the Black Pearl* (2003)

2006 Nominated, *Charlie and the Chocolate Factory* (2005)

2007 Nominated, *Pirates of the Caribbean: Dead Man's Chest* (2006)

2008 Won, *Sweeney Todd: The Demon Barber of Fleet Street* (2007)

Golden Globe for Best Performance by an Actor in a Motion Picture—Drama

2005 Nominated, *Finding Neverland* (2004)

Screen Actors Guild Award for Outstanding Performance by a Male Actor in a Leading Role

2004 Won, *Pirates of the Caribbean: The Curse of the Black Pearl* (2003)

2005 Nominated, *Finding Neverland* (2004)

Golden Palm, Cannes Film Festival

1997 Nominated, *The Brave* (1997)

Further Reading

Heard, Christopher. *Johnny Depp Photo Album*. London: Plexus, 2007.

Johnstone, Nick. *Johnny Depp: The Illustrated Biography*. London: Carlton Publishing Group, 2006.

Robb, Brian. *Johnny Depp: A Modern Rebel*. London: Plexus, 2006

Singer, Michael. *Bring Me That Horizon: The Making of Pirates of the Caribbean*. New York: Disney Editions, 2007.

Internet Resources

http://www.deppimpact.com

A Web site with information about Johnny, including a biography, list of his films, and links to interviews.

http://johnnydepp.com

A Web site devoted to all aspects of Johnny's career, with background information as well as daily updates.

http://johnnydeppweb.com

This Web site features an extensive collection of information related to the life and career of Johnny Depp.

Glossary

agent—the person responsible for the business dealings of an actor, writer, director, or artist.

biopic—a film biography; a motion picture that tells the story of a person's life.

blockbuster—a very popular and financially successful movie.

director—the person in charge of guiding actors in their performances and coordinating filming.

episode—each of a series of segments presented in a television or radio show.

gonzo journalism—a style of journalism in which reporters include personal feelings and opinions.

Oscar—nickname for the golden statuette given annually at the Academy Awards by the Academy of Motion Picture Arts and Sciences in recognition of excellence.

paparazzi—freelance photographers who aggressively pursue celebrities for the purpose of taking candid photographs.

pilot—in television, a program made to test audience reaction in order to determine whether to produce the program as a series.

premiere—the first public showing of a movie or opening of a performance.

producer—the person responsible for hiring actors to work on a movie, obtaining financing, and making sure the film is made.

sequel—a published, broadcast, or recorded work that continues a story that began in a previous work, generally using many of the same characters.

Chapter Notes

p. 6: "On one level, I was . . ." Erik Hedegaard, "Johnny Darko," *Rolling Stone* (February 10, 2005), 52.

p. 10: "forced into the role . . ." Bruce Kirkland, "A Pirate's Life for Depp," *Calgary Sun* (July 2, 2006).

p. 11: "Please, don't let . . ." Hedegaard, *Rolling Stone*, 53.

p. 11: "When I didn't win . . ." Hedegaard, *Rolling Stone*, 53.

p. 14: "When I was growing up . . ." Jan Janssen, "Interview," *Hello* (November 2, 1999).

p. 14: "I always felt like . . ." Christopher Heard, *Depp* (Toronto, Canada: ECW Press, 2001), 3.

p. 14: "My body is a journal . . ." Chris Heath, "Portrait of the Oddest as a Young Man," *Details* (May 1993).

p. 14: "My mom and my dad . . ." Gavin Edwards, "Johnny Depp Sings," *Rolling Stone* (January 24, 2008), 36.

p. 15: "When I was about . . ." Edwards, *Rolling Stone*, 36.

p. 15: "When I left high school . . ." Heard, *Depp*, 9.

p. 17: "I was married when . . ." Holly Millea, "Ghost in the Machine," *Premiere* (February 1995), 50.

p. 20: "I cut most of . . ." Christopher Heard, ed. *Johnny Depp: Photo Album* (London: Plexus, 2007), 19.

p. 22: "Hanson is not someone . . ." Brian J. Robb, *Johnny Depp: A Modern Rebel* (London: Plexus, 2006), 25–26.

p. 24: "The series was great training . . ." Glenn Collins, "Johnny Depp Contemplates Life As, and After, 'Scissorhands,'" *New York Times* (January 10, 1991), C17.

p. 28: "It wasn't similar to anything . . ." Collins, *New York Times*.

p. 30: "covering his face with scars . . . Chris Nashawaty, "Johnny Depp and Tim Burton: A DVD Report Card," EW.com, March 30, 2008. http://www.ew.com/ew/gallery/0,,20186999_1,00.html

p. 30: "I hope this won't sound . . ." Collins, *New York Times*.

p. 31: "great character actor in a . . ." Elaine Lipworth, "The Biggest Outsider of Them All," *The Independent* (July 7, 2006).

p. 33: "For a few years . . ." Joey Berlin, *Toxic Fame* (Detroit: Visible Ink Press, 1996), 113.

p. 34: "That was kind of a . . ." Hedegaard, *Rolling Stone*, 53.

p. 35: "Maybe I'm a dummy . . ." Chris Nashawaty, "A Head of Its Time," *Entertainment Weekly* (November 19, 1999), 38.

p. 36: "Johnny enjoys losing himself . . ." Nancy Mills, "Fears & Longing in Johnny Depp: Fresh from His Wild Hunter Thompson Role, the Actor's Ready to Grow Up," *Daily News* (May 17, 1998).

p. 37: "As of May 27 . . ." Heard, ed. *Johnny Depp: Photo Album*, 82.

p. 39: "I thought it was funny . . ." Robb, *Johnny Depp: A Modern Rebel*, 139.

p. 39: "meaningful way for Depp fans . . ." "Johnny's Angels: Depp Fans for Charity" June 15, 2008. http://www.johnnysangels.org/

p. 43: "Crazy for Johnny . . . " Anthony Breznican, *USA Today* (July 10, 2006), 01D.

Index

Numbers in **bold italics** refer to captions.

Photo Credits

About the Author

BILL WINE is a freelance writer specializing in entertainment. He teaches film at La Salle University in Philadelphia and serves as the movie critic for KYW Newsradio. He lives in Wyncote, Pennsylvania, with his wife Suzanne and has two daughters, Simone and Paulina.